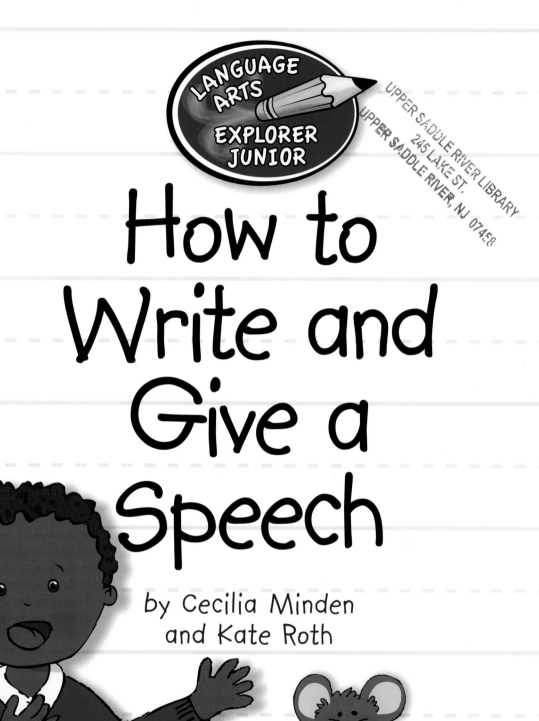

LANGUAGE ARTS
EXPLORER
JUNIOR

How to Write and Give a Speech

by Cecilia Minden
and Kate Roth

CHERRY LAKE PUBLISHING · ANN ARBOR, MICHIGAN

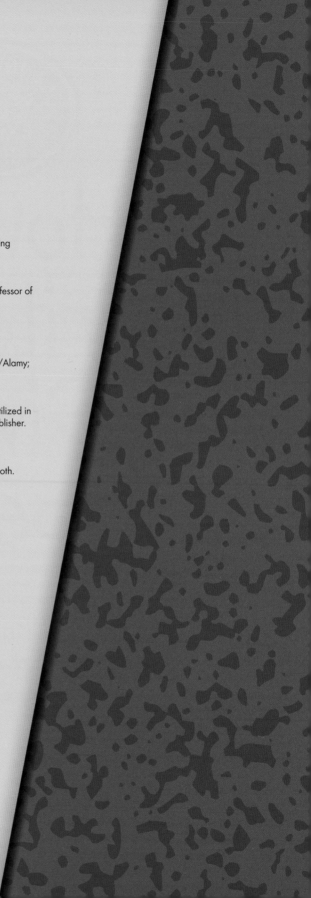

Published in the United States of America by Cherry Lake Publishing
Ann Arbor, Michigan
www.cherrylakepublishing.com

Content Adviser: Jeannette Mancilla-Martinez, EdD, Assistant Professor of
Literacy, Language, and Culture, University of Illinois at Chicago

Design and Illustration: The Design Lab

Photo Credits: Page 5, ©Andrey Lipko/Shutterstock, Inc.; page 6,
©iStockphoto.com/MichaelDeLeon; page 13, ©Myrleen Pearson/Alamy;
page 16, ©Photos 12/Alamy

Library of Congress Cataloging-in-Publication Data
Minden, Cecilia.
  How to write and give a speech/by Cecilia Minden and Kate Roth.
     p. cm.–(Language arts explorer junior)
  Includes bibliographical references and index.
  ISBN-13: 978-1-61080-108-9 (lib. bdg.)
  ISBN-13: 978-1-61080-280-2 (pbk.)
  1. Speechwriting–Juvenile literature. 2. Public speaking–Juvenile
literature. I. Roth, Kate. II. Title.
  PN4142.M56 2011
  808.5–dc22   2011004021

Cherry Lake Publishing would like to acknowledge the work
of The Partnership for 21st Century Skills. Please visit
www.21stcenturyskills.org for more information.

Printed in the United States of America
Corporate Graphics Inc.
July 2011
CLFA09

Table of Contents

I Have to Give a Speech!

You might give many speeches as you grow older.

Many people are scared of giving a **speech**. There is no need to be scared. With a little planning, you can give a speech with **confidence**!

First, ask yourself a few questions. Why are you giving this speech? Is it for a class project? Is it for a club or sports team? Knowing the **purpose** of the speech helps you plan what you want to say.

Think carefully about what your speech will cover.

CHAPTER TWO

Speak About What You Know!

Always keep your audience in mind when writing a speech.

Giving a speech is one way of sharing what you know with others. Speeches are different than reports. People read written reports. They listen to speeches. Think about how you speak to others as you write your speech. Keep your sentences short. Choose your words carefully.

Too many details make it hard for the **audience** to keep up with you.

Let's say you are asked to give a 3- to 5-minute speech to your class. How will you choose a topic? It is always best to talk about what you know. Why not write about a favorite hobby or activity?

ACTIVITY

Choose a Topic!

HERE'S WHAT YOU'LL NEED:
- A pencil and paper (or a computer and a printer)

INSTRUCTIONS:
1. Make a list of your favorite hobbies or activities.
2. Choose one hobby or activity for your speech.
3. Now list everything that is interesting about the hobby or activity.
4. Read over this second list. What points would interest your classmates most?

Speech Topic Ideas:
1. Hiking
2. Playing the guitar
3. Playing basketball

Sample List of Topics

Interesting things about hiking:
1. What hikers wear
2. How hikers carry supplies
3. Hiking safely
4. Good hiking spots
5. Reading maps

CHAPTER THREE

Get Their Attention

Some speakers begin their speech with an interesting fact or a story. Others begin with a quote or a question. These are all ways you can get the audience's **attention**.

You should also tell the audience what your speech will be about. It is important to include why they should listen to your talk.

ACTIVITY

Write the Opening!

HERE'S WHAT YOU'LL NEED:
- Books or articles about your topic
- A pencil and paper (or a computer and a printer)

INSTRUCTIONS:
1. Read books, articles, or Web sites that deal with your topic. Use what you learn to create a list of different ways to open your speech.
2. Find a quote about your topic and write it down.
3. Pick an interesting fact about your topic and write it down.
4. Come up with a question about your topic and write it down.
5. Look over your list and choose the best way to open your speech. Start writing!

Sample List of Openings

QUOTE:
"Make your feet your friend."—J. M. Barrie

INTERESTING FACT:
Hiking is called "hill walking" in England.

QUESTION:
How many of you like to sleep late on Saturdays?

Sample Opening Statement

How many of you like to sleep late on Saturdays? I do, too!
One Saturday a month, though, I get up early.
Why? That is the day my family goes hiking in the
woods. Today, I will tell you a few things about hiking.

CHAPTER FOUR

Building the Body of Your Speech

You have the audience's attention! Now you must write the **body** of your speech. Choose three main points about your topic that you plan to discuss.

First, name the points. Then tell more about each of them. This helps the audience follow your speech. Think about the order of your main points. As you write, try to link the main points together.

A map would be a good visual aid for a speech about faraway places.

You may want to use **visual aids**. Make sure that everyone in the audience will be able to see the visual aids. Do not pass around objects during your speech. Sometimes the audience pays more attention to the objects than to the speaker!

Write the Body!

HERE'S WHAT YOU'LL NEED:
- A pencil and paper (or a computer and a printer)

INSTRUCTIONS:
1. Write the three main points you want to put in your speech.
2. Explain the first point.
3. Explain the second point.
4. Explain the third point.
5. Read aloud what you've written. Does it make sense? Will your audience understand?

Sample Points to Put in the Body

Ideas for the body of the speech:
1. What to wear when hiking
2. What to carry when hiking
3. How to stay safe while hiking

Sample Explanation of a Main Point

First, here are some ideas about what to wear when hiking. Keep in mind that you may be walking several miles. It is important to wear comfortable shoes with closed toes. I like to wear thick socks. Hiking shoes and socks protect your feet. I also wear a hat to protect my face from the sun.

CHAPTER FIVE

Wrapping Everything Up

A strong ending to your speech helps the audience remember what you have said. You should repeat your main points. Some speakers even repeat their opening lines to bring the speech "full circle." Finally, always thank the audience for listening to you.

Good speeches keep the audience interested from beginning to end.

Write the Ending!

HERE'S WHAT YOU'LL NEED:
- A pencil and paper (or a computer and a printer)

INSTRUCTIONS:
1. Restate the main points of your speech.
2. Write a strong final sentence. One idea is to repeat your opening lines.
3. Thank your audience.

Sample Ending

Now you know a few things about hiking in the woods. You know what to wear, what to bring with you, and how to stay safe. Finally, always remember not to leave anything behind. Take out whatever you bring into the woods. Leave the trails clear for animals and other hikers. Thank you.

CHAPTER SIX

Practice, Practice, Practice!

You finished writing your speech! Now you need to **rehearse** it out loud. Some speakers use small note cards to help them remember key points. Just try to speak naturally.

You should also practice with your visual aids. Remember to look at the audience and not the visual aids. You may want to invite friends and family members to listen to you practice. They can tell you what they think and offer suggestions. Ask them to time you if you have been given a time limit. Make sure your speech does not run over the limit!

Practicing will make you more confident. You will soon discover that speaking in front of an audience is fun. Giving speeches helps you learn skills that you will use for the rest of your life!

Rehearse!

HERE'S WHAT YOU'LL NEED:
- A copy of your speech
- A pencil
- Note cards
- Any visual aids

INSTRUCTIONS:
1. Write the opening of your speech on a note card.
2. Write each of the three main points on separate note cards.
3. Write the ending on a note card.
4. Write what visual aids you want to use and when.
5. Rehearse your speech several times using the note cards and visual aids. Ask friends and family members to listen to you and time you!

Sample Note Card

Main point #2:

What to carry when hiking

Remember to show the audience the water bottle and map after discussing this point!

ACTIVITY

Make Sure You Didn't Miss Anything!

Ask yourself these questions as you rehearse your speech:

☐ YES ☐ NO Do I have an attention-getting opening?

☐ YES ☐ NO Do I tell the audience what my speech is about in the opening?

☐ YES ☐ NO Do I limit myself to discussing three main points?

☐ YES ☐ NO Do I give examples or explanations for each of the main points?

☐ YES ☐ NO Do I repeat the main points in the end?

☐ YES ☐ NO Do I have a strong ending that helps the audience remember what I said?

☐ YES ☐ NO Do I remember to thank the audience?

☐ YES ☐ NO Do I stay within my time limit?

☐ YES ☐ NO Do I know when and where to include my visual aids?

Glossary

attention (uh-TEN-shuhn) the act of looking at and listening to a speaker

audience (AW-dee-uhntz) a group of listeners

body (BAH-dee) the main part of a speech

confidence (KAN-fuh-duhntz) believing in yourself and your ability to achieve something

purpose (PUHR-puhs) goal

rehearse (ri-HURSE) practice

speech (SPEECH) a planned presentation before an audience

topic (TAH-pik) subject

visual aids (VIH-zhu-uhl AYDZ) materials that the audience can look at during a speech

For More Information

BOOKS

Bullard, Lisa. *Ace Your Oral or Multimedia Presentation*. Berkeley Heights, NJ: Enslow Publishers, 2009.

WEB SITES

Best-Speech-Topics.com—Speech Topics for Kids
www.best-speech-topics.com/speech-topics-for-kids.html
Check out this Web site for countless cool speech subjects!

Famous Speeches and Speech Topics
http://www.famous-speeches-and-speech-topics.info/
Visit this site to check out famous speeches as well as additional tips on public speaking.

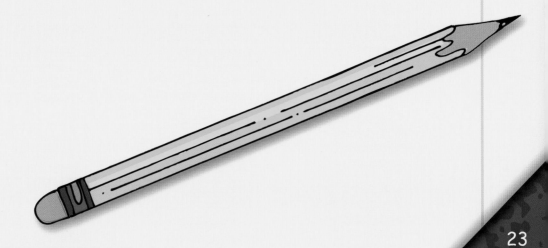

Index

About the Authors

Cecilia Minden, PhD, is the former director of the Language and Literacy Program at Harvard Graduate School of Education. She earned her doctorate from the University of Virginia. While at Harvard, Dr. Minden also taught several writing courses. Her research focuses on early literacy skills and developing phonics curriculums. She is now a full-time literacy consultant and the author of more than 100 books for children. Dr. Minden lives with her family in Chapel Hill, North Carolina. She likes to write early in the morning while the house is still quiet.

Kate Roth has a doctorate from Harvard University in language and literacy and a master's degree from Columbia University Teachers College in curriculum and teaching. Her work focuses on writing instruction in the primary grades. She has taught kindergarten, first grade, and Reading Recovery. She has also instructed hundreds of teachers around the world in early-literacy practices. She lives in Shanghai, China, with her husband and three children, ages 2, 6, and 9. Together they do a lot of writing to stay in touch with friends and family and to record their experiences.